A LOGGER'S WORLD

A COLLECTION

Other Books by Don Davison

An Outline of a Philosophy of the Consciousness of Truth
The Concept of Personhood in the Evolutionary Process of Being
The Game of Life: A Player's Manual for Executives and Others
A Novela: The Gift

Social and Political Commentary

Sign Posts: A Collection of Essays,
  Volumes I–VII

Poetry

Thoughts and Feelings Book I
Thoughts and Feelings Book II
Needles from the Ponderosas at Zirahuen
Seeds from the Ponderosas at Zirahuen
Pitch from the Ponderosas at Zirahuen
Humus from the Ponderosas at Zirahuen
Sawdust from the Ponderosas at Zirahuen
Sun's Rays Bouncing off the Ponderosas at Zirahuen
Shadows Beneath the Ponderosas at Zirahuen
Cones from the Ponderosas at Zirahuen
Pollen Sifting from the Ponderosas at Zirahuen
Reflections from Lucerne
Searching Swamps
Questions
Time's Echoes
Memories
Insistences
Splashes
Ripples
Pebbles
McAlpine Camp
Shoreline
Vales and Rills

Collections

Always Extolling
Murmurings
Iris and Other Things
Pieces of the Journey
Through the Swamps of Time
Reflections from Lucerne
The Twelfth Hour
Pebbles on the Shore
Still Water

A LOGGER'S WORLD

A COLLECTION

by Don Davison

Zirahuen Publishers

ISBN 978-0-9858130-8-6

Cover photo by Don Davison
Author photo by Patricia Davison

A special thanks to Louella Holter.

And again –
to Patricia for everything.

CONTENTS

MIND WORK

Why is it that I am so surprised,
when I stumble upon the threshold of my wonder?
Awe leaps into eyes and ears so often
I get exhausted saying,
"Wow!"
And then too,
there are those moments
when lights flash,
sparks fly, bells ring, heart is warmed
and I realize
I have come to know something new.
A mind is snapped to attention.
From anywhere something
enters its resting place and says,
"Ah ha!"

AGAIN

Some time ago it was written
– we "cracked the cosmic egg."
Following those cracks,
we delved into the mystic's paths.
"Where to now?"
we ask our sodden hearts
bound in the implosive centripetal
currents of our times.
We choose and choose and choose,
driven by a frozen hope.
We pant and race against the pace.
Then,
in those founded moments of repose
from Nature's prevailing silence,
we feel and hear the voice of God,
"Come follow me!"
And like those twelve so long ago
– enraptured by the Holy Spirit –
we set ourselves
– again –
to walk the path of life.
To our lost brothers and sisters,
we are obligated to shake the cosmic dust
from our sandals.
Opening our drooping eyes
and weary hearts we take up
– again –
the mantel of a "second religiousness."

– Again –
we begin
– again –
to heroically love our neighbors as ourselves.

A WRITER

No man is who you think he may be behind the pen.
There are always those primeval traces
coursing through his veins
affecting the screens of the eyes and the mind.
And the caldrons,
from which boil and splash his emotions,
are fed by fires within
that rage and subside
like the rise and the lowering of the tides.
And yet,
there is that other admixture of swirlings
of faith and hope,
comingled with charity,
that bubbles forth
from the end of his searing pen.

SELF-SPEAK

Self-speak, left to itself,
is of little help to one or another.
That there is a need for reflections,
history speaks volumes.
It is, indeed,
worth the efforts to lay down one's mullings
on the matters of life.
It seems to me:
the efforts of unbridled enthusiasm
are both good and bad.
Good –
in that it can lead to an expression of a free choice,
which may in time,
prove to be of some worth.
Bad –
in the sense that without prior knowledge
the fullness of consequences may not be foreseen.
In the great movement of births, deaths,
and the layering of time,
there is always the presence of a naiveté that,
without further experience,
can lead to the accumulation of ignorance.
Nature's omnipresence dictum:
Pay attention of die![1]
in the presence of abundance
does not weigh heavily enough.
Each succeeding generation
moves away from the efforts of the many
who have toiled to make in their self-expressions
a better life for self and others.

---

[1] See "Pay Attention Or Die!" reprinted later in this volume.

It is only with sufficient heft,
and gravity of consequences,
that we are forced to take note
and choose other actions.
Habits can breed contempt for the necessity of growth.
It is in this vein that the young,
and those who eschew reflection,
are always in danger of a stasis of thought.
It can bring about a friction with the facts
that ignites reflection on those unattended actions.

HUMAN PROGRESS

The wind has left the sails.
It has been puffing only intermittently
for some time,
really forever.
We must take out the oars
and press our wills
into the service of our intentions.
To take this barque on liberty's journey
there must always be a sufficient number
to man the oars
or we will all succumb
to Nature's foibles.
Make way!
Make straight the way
to hallowed ground
where Freedom's gifts to us abound.

HOPE EXPRESSED

In the now-known undulations
of the All,[1]
we feel and hear the whisperings
of the Heart of God.
Beneath the crust,
laborings move us towards one another.
The blue-green presence of algae congeals
and spreads tentacles
in the almost-silence,
achieving crescendos of yesnesses
becoming words morphing to flesh.
We touch one another
in depths we do not yet fathom
as variegated columnnals spring into pedicels
and peduncles emerge, thrusting presences[2]
in an effervescence of
Moving Lovingness.
Holding it all together,
explosions and implosions,
breathe in their googolplex infinitude
singing His Name,
"I am who am."

---

[1] The recent confirmations of our striding ambitions to know more of Him have resulted in our ability to see, hear, and know the particle-waves of gravity and so much more.

[2] As life shares itself (*Still Water, A Collection*), we must always honor the presence of every aspect.

And we,
we sense the abundance of Spirit
as the process of
It/We becoming I/We[1]
shares its abundance.
Our lives are spent re-cognizing
His Face
across the surface of eternal time,
as the Never Alone spreads charity
again and again forever and ever.
Amen.

---

[1] "To Dream (It/We – I/We)" first appeared in *Sign Posts, Volume VI.*

HEY!

It's raining!
What delight!
Droplets and puddles
radiating centricity.
Waves and ripples
– undulations –
that in their quiescence,
provide mirrors of floating clouds
in which I see
the efforts of the All.

GOD FINDING ME

It is in the soft contemplation
of a vast conflagration
– the heavens themselves –
(and a roaring hearth)
that we are set still enough
to see and to sense
the strength of the necessity
of an eternal will
that forms a formless sea
birthing essential things,
drawing me into Itself.

NEVER JUST NOISE

The hammer strikes the anvil of my mind
and the ringing
echoes in the recesses of my memories
from which I pull forth
the essence of my presence.

LIVES ON THE EDGES

An honest movement of the species
is a democratic jihad.
Life lives on the edges of the interface.
A fight for one's own self,
family and land is different
from just fighting a war of ideology.
And so ours is a land of democracy.
We will never give in or give up.
Freedom is our clarion.
The human family journey
is not unlike that of a military family
– moving in the wake of a career
from war to war for self and others –
giving us all an opportunity
to freely participate
in our own war.

JUDGEMENT'S SEAT

Beware the blindness of an age!
– of bygone eras,
of our current confluence,
and of those to come.
Be not seduced by static visions!
Judge not by old facts,
when new ones mount so quickly.
Be nimble of mind and heart
in appraisals of the newness and the oldness
in thoughts and deeds.
Choose wisely
in the movements and moments of the present.
We must continue to recall:
"As it was in the beginning is now and ever shall be."
Simple truths bedeck each syllable of time.
It is all One and I am only one.

TIME MOVES ON

In the exuberance of youth
flushed with passion
– I met her!
Fifty-three years on …
in the gentle silence of her presence,
and the distilled wisdom of reflection,
she is found again!

THIN SLICES
(My conundrum with the accumulation
of history's efforts.)

Not of before
– something here now –
really mine,
(but not really)
only templates of "my time"
(but not *mine* really).
I watched and I learned.
But they weren't *really mine.*
Mine was *mine*
and I don't really know how to
make sense of the slices
when they go and come
and some of them
(or pieces from them)
form a part of what I think
my life should be;
when what I need is to be connected
to *my before, my now,*
and what I earnestly hope will become
a part of *my future.*
But how will I know
– *really know* –
if they are only slices,
just shadows of life's Grand Halo,
when *mine* is only *mine* and not
someone else's?

How is it that *my* judgment of truths
will come home to *me*
and form a part of *my* forevers,
when only thin and ever more thinning slices
float across my horizons and I
– in moving on –
cannot get from them that golden thread
that ties *my me* to *myself*
and to *my* God?

OUR TASK

It is always our task
to re-member, to re-construct
our humanity
as we move from arid seasons
to abundance.
In all of this we must never forget
the bitter taste of a thought,
the piercing of the eye with an abhorrent screen,
a piteous murmur shattering silence,
screams of terror.
Somehow,
we must have sufficient cohesion,
the glue providing the threads
to hold it all together.
Virtue where art thou?

WHERE AM I? WHERE IS IT?

We delve into delicious flights of fancy.
Imagination opens its doors and we risk it all.
The savory freedom of purpose and intent
grabs our souls and we succumb
to a search for hidden treasure.
What great needs bend the iron of our hearts
and take us into realms wished for,
hoped for,
sought after?
How is it that a vision so clear emerges
from the turmoil of reality
and settles in tranquil reveries?
And why is it that a gentleness
covers everything, hard or soft?
Lost upon a range of fertile vistas,
we gladly spend our hours hiding
from God's plan,
or is it when we are so enthralled that
we find ourselves strolling in His Garden
in misty mornings and dappled afternoons?
Are these the times when we vaguely see
through the thin film of the present
and gaze upon eternal truths
that light flames birthing dreams?

OUR NOW

If one does anything
and does not have a religious commitment
to one's own life
– there is no lasting fundamental commitment to any life.
Out of the fatigue of time
– from the wavering luminosity of spirit –
come the images of those who have gone before,
those who will come after.
It is for all of the intrepid souls,
those who have gone before
steadfastly into the winds of time,
that we are obligated to do our very best
in everything we do.
From what deep well of soul scratching
will sufficient courage surge up
to do the right thing?

EVERY LIFE

Every life – A prayer,
whispered,
screamed,
spoken,
mumbled,
shouted,
offered.

VIRTUE'S POND

What mitochondrial trail
links us to a path called good?
Deep in the heart of humanity,
amidst the poundings of our rage,
we wonder how deep the pond of virtue.
Is it that trails of our history pooled
and birthed sufficient care,
emerging to own its own still reflections
in shattered shards of wisdom
streaking across our minds?
And how is it that we have a sense
of responsibility for most of us
and other things?
From what vistas do we see enshrined
a second look
respecting all we know?
And how does love burst forth from chaos,
or is that just our mistaken point of view?
Is it that between the thump, thump, thump
of our pounding racing hearts
those tiny interstitials of silence
lay bare our wonder for all who care to see?

I must know me.
I must know you.
I must know Him.

THE DAWN RISES

The dawn rises again
from the depths of nocturnal quiescence
and stretching itself across the sky
raises the heads of the drooping daisies
gracing the fields.
Another day says,
"Yes!"
to the world.
From the darkest shadows of the night
emerges the brilliant colors of the day.[1]

---

[1] "Dawn Rises" first appeared in *Collections: Still Water*, published in 2015.

AGE WEARS

Age wears the stone.
Gentle movements of the seasons
nudge, chip, scrape, abrade
the surface.
All wearing a bit away
until that very last crystalline grain
of quartz
rolls its way downriver
and splits into infinitesimal shards
that dissolve
in the onslaught
of water, light, and time …
A life is gone.
Where is it that soul maintains?

PAY ATTENTION OR DIE![1]

From the plethora of the plasticities of the age,
we must shelter ourselves
and immerse ourselves.
And yet,
beware the eclectic dynamic that creates
a pseudo frenzy disturbing all those
who have not been able to see
the infinitesimal enclaves
available to every seeking soul!
Serenity reigns!
As every coin of truth has two sides:
Nature's omnipresent mandate:
"Pay attention or die!"
elicits, of necessity,
the need for those essential pauses,
the ones that apprehend the sacred stillness
of the now,
letting us "know" the peaceful pathways
of the Divinity's open arms
and gentle voice saying,
"Be still and come to me,
I am always and forever with you."

---

[1] This poem first appeared in *Collection: Still Water*, published in 2015.

BALTIMORE[1]

Only a tiny glint of a reflection
– hints of trouble.
There is a shuddering in my soul.
How thin the water on the land?
Most has been wicked away.
Should we be concerned
that it will all be gone
leaving only barren ground?
Too little have we done
to preserve the sacredness of Nature.
We have ridden rough-shod
over her breasts and shoulders:
desecrated vales,
squandered time.
We have bred wolf pups
and abandoned them to themselves.
We have failed ourselves and future generations.
Woe be unto us (USA)!
Smoldering remnants
of a once vibrant culture
slip into time,
leaving tracks of decadence
scattered in the shoals
of our forgotten
and abandoned responsibilities.
We see the crops of Baltimore
raging in the streets.
Must we only stand stupefied and watch?
Are there are no leaders left?

---

[1] From *Sign Posts, A Collection of Essays, Volume VI.*

WHAT HAVE WE DONE?

We teach the young to be cynics –
when they should be looking for a deeper
understanding of compassion.
This is our greatest lie.
Yet, it is done!
When my part slips into the "Whole"
and I know it,
then too,
I know that I am known.
The serenity of it All empties Itself
into me and I into It.
Time stops as It all becomes a yes!
There is no-thing anymore
– It is become,
and in that intensity of "I am!"
I am enveloped in the cloud
of the Known–Unknowing.
It is done![1]

---

[1]This is the gift that we should be giving to the young. Shame on us for the lies
we have told.

ALWAYS WOLVES

The wolves of history
fed upon corpses of lives lost
to the perfidy of ideologies.
"An endangered species?" some say.
I say, "No!"
We now have an abundance of human wolves.
Listen to the howlings of the winds.
They carry the wailings
of suffering souls as an ever more
pernicious humanity prowls the earth.

A MOMENT OF SHARING

A voice said,
"You are my image and likeness.
I love you so that you can love yourself."
So, we have:
"The word became flesh.
Take this and eat of it for it is my gift to you."
And so it is that we have become
the "gifted ones" –
those that already have that which always is.
There was only left to say "Amen"
and yet,
because It is the "Yes" of the All,
It is – everything of and for the All.
I stood con-fused in my self-knowing.
Then, He also said,
"I am always more than.
You are always more than."
I could only utter in reply,
"Into your hands I commend my spirit."
And as this was whispered,
I heard Him say,
"You are already in the spirit.
You are the beforehand of and with the Father."
Yet for me,
the con-fusion of the I is that of all-ways being
a 'Yes!'
Again,
all that I could say was,
"Abba! Father! Thank you!"

LEST WE FORGET

We are not fighting against ISIS –
they are poor souls left to God's mercy –
we are fighting for the innocent,
the forgotten.
To them we owe the gift of hope.

I LIVE

I live the struggle of purgatory.
I sing the eternal song:
"I live!"
I live in an *arrebatado*[1] of the mind.
I live in an aging body.
I live with a loving heart.
I live!

---

[1] *Arrebatado* means "whirlwind/impassioned."

MY GOD! MY GOD!

Thank you for giving my me to me,
for in so doing,
giving me to myself,
I have learned to love the tree,
and in so doing,
have given myself to Thee!

HERE WE HAVE IT![1]

The dissonance of the age
gives us examples of
horrifically dishonest people.
They may "believe" that
their misdeeds are "right"
when indeed they are wrong.
Any point of departure concerning
one's life perspective
that does not lead to a betterment
of individual potential
gives awareness of an opportunity
to responsibly become more than they/them,
my brothers and my sisters were,
even more than they are,
is withholding life from the innocent.
Compassion based on a new truth,
on an ever new individual potential
opens realms of new responsibilities.
This is the only true human interchange.
Lies steal truth!
Do not bear false witness!
Do not steal truth's freedom and responsibility.
That is stealing one's own ability to choose.
We must renew the existential opportunities
for each and every one
– to the degree that they are able.

---

[1] To remove the Ten Commandments from public space is a sacrilege of the greatest proportion.

Keep to the Pilgrim Road.
Be on the Pilgrim way.
Allow for each to move towards a choice of one,
to be reaching out one's hand to God,
all/ways saying "Yes to life!"
An infinite and forever "Yes to love!"

MEGA MOLECULES

Mega molecules
of strength and power
are now exerting an indelible influence
in our everyday lives.
We have become the super-connected
organic whole of our planet home.
I am reminded,
again,
as I hear the sweet melody of a redwing blackbird,
that even tweets affect their surrounds.
And then,
I think of the legions
(swarms if you will)
of integrated drones,
every variety:
information, cargo, energy,
and munitions of ultra-light smart potentials,
an ad infinitum
of essential surgically aided tools
to conduct operations
that will target
the problematics of our current age.
All are here now
as a part of the arsenal of human protection.
We have arrived
full-blown
in our existential moment.

LIGHTS OUT!

A match seduces the wick
and by the soft light of the candle
I see the hidden faint
shadows of the day
emerge in the "there"
of a glowing presence.
Then,
and along with the gentle flickerings
on the floor in front of the fireplace,
I also hear so clearly the wind's wailings.
All is well,
even better than before.[1]

---

[1] "Lights Out!" first appeared in *Shoreline*, by Don Davison.

LIVING TODAY

Light is hard. Dark is soft.
The double helix of our biology
now shows itself at the cosmic level.
The woof and weave
of thought in all things
manifests itself as one of infinite parts,
all interrelated in ways
that we are just beginning to fathom.
We now use the word "smart" attached to everything –
homes, cars, phones, refrigerators –
well,
just about everything.
We even now speak to each other,
and ourselves,
with the cryptic emphatic
"Think smarter!"
as we attempt to assemble
the available procedural tools of our time.
"Use the Net! Look it up!"
"Networking is where it's at" –
ostensibly where we are!
Our environment shows itself,
and ourselves,
as an integrated whole.
And yes,
we have archaic parts –
I may even be one of them –
age, you know.
I lag behind my own progeny
in understanding
the new potentials of "information."

Often,
when pondering with my grandchildren,
I hear,
"Grampa!
Look it up!"
Still,
I remember that learning curve of experience
as I maturated into my adulating phase.
That insightful idea,
those sparks of thought that arrested me
and served themselves
as consequential
in my patterns of thinking
and reflective reposes:
"Will it fit in the sequence of the real?"
"Is it moral?"
always flowed through and about
my flashing of thoughts.
And yes,
there were those times,
when in haste,
I pressed the wrong button
and deleted everything
– and then hunted for
"previous strokes"
to regain my sense of thought.
How seductive PDAs have become.
In their efficient
nanosecond way
they have recast our expectations.

Today,
in my mundane moments,
I am reminded that all things move,
caps, valves, lines,
all exposed to internal and external variations –
one of the latter,
a curious and mischievous malamute puppy –
all will have their say
in the context of my world:
an irrigation system,
quite large,
spanning my six-acre country farm
suffers the vagaries of
water, wind, and animals.
In the midst of it all,
I try to put words to paper.
Words,
that written today as insightful,
may become the hum-drum straw
of tomorrow.
I attempt to settle myself
and capture my current musings.
Meanwhile,
feeling that always omnipresent
passage of time,
as it pushes and nudges me through my days,
I value the treasures of my life.
Hurry, scurry, wonder, worry,
salt themselves
in my thoughts of beauty and wonder
and plague my waking
and dreaming hours.

Yet,
the sun still sets in blazes of glory
lasting but briefly,
and I,
I am awe-struck
drinking my full measure.
Alas,
all things move and so too must I
(as I remind myself of Rule #2 in
The Game of Life[1])
"Stand Still in Silence!
So that you can apprehend
the meaning of it all."

---

[1] *The Game of Life: A Player's Manual for Executives and Others* is available at Amazon.com, like all of Dr. Davison's works.

JOHN KEATS

Words brooding restless scenes
become a focused frenzy rolling on and on
smashing and crushing invincible
enclaves of silence.
A tortured tongue labors thoughts
to visions of soulful dirges
giving somber notes of Nature's
headlong efforts.
History's machinations muddle
senses lost from moorings too slight
to hold a single thought.
Always there was, always there is,
the spray and foam of more than
and less than that leaves us bobbing
in endless waves.
Only an open eye, an open heart,
can bear out in time of breath and water
all constructs in the hours of our days.
We weep and laugh, and wonder too,
what makes us rise to the unknown
efforts of each new day?

THIN SLICES # 2 OF OUR NOW
(More conundrums with the accumulation
of history's efforts.)

Life is that thin, thin slip of an instant.
And that is all.
From the cacklings of the dawn
to the whisperings of the vespers,
from the cluttered thought conversations
of the mind's ruminations,
I must take leave.
The door is open.
The setting sun beckons.
My time is coming.
My time is going.
That there are always some places
and always some times seems obvious.
Something else is in the swilling of the now.
It moves from the then to the not yet forever
in that flux of eternal movement.
There is always that presence:
A being becoming;
the parts and the whole,
the whole and the parts.
In the warping reciprocity
of the physics of our day,
we must allow
for a deep-seated craving after truth.
That there is always a greater truth
has become self-manifest:
Share everything![1]

---

[1] This poem also appears *in Sign Posts, Volume VII.*

A REFLECTION

Beware the weariness of the mind
as it peers into the mirror
of our reflections.
Be on guard against
the supposed druthers
of our youthful exaggerations.
The ones we used
to create our self-image,
the ones we harbored
for a lifetime
and used as a bastion,
with the vagaries of circumstance,
while we were confronted
with our limitations
and our accumulated deeds
both done and only hoped for.

A THOUGHT – AND A CONCLUSION

After much rumination,
I slipped silently from the forest
and stood upon the headlands
peering at a raging sea.
I wondered,
"From what whirlpool of efforts
does enough grace come
to calm the waters?"
I, too,
whether brother or sister,
wear sandals in my search.
He gives to each
a layered piece of His Great Garden,
to do His will
as it messes with our own.

BE AWARE!

When is our life an easy set of circumstances?
When the silent whirlpool eases off
into a calm stream
and we float and wonder what caught us
and held us for that brief moment.
It is in our recollection
that we are caught and loosened.
By whom do the vagaries of time
sway back and forth?
"We know so little and pretend so much,"
has been written.
Of a time we all come to know,
"*We* must ride, always aware, and always ready."

A VISION

What is a vision of freedom worth?
A fighting will that says,
"Remember the power of the known unknown
and the power of the unknown known."
One cannot be half-assed about the rule of law:
The spirit and the letter
is never enough without the heart.

PASSING BY

We move
from unsettled
to riddled,
from frenetic
to hectic,
from how people choose to live
to understanding what we give,
from nuts and bolts that come loose
to errant synapses that cook the goose.
We've finally arrived.
Now we're all hived.
Sickened,
we know what we rate:
an utterly dishonest and dysfunctional state.

WHOSE NATURE?

From out of the silence in the forest primeval
come the roaring bear and the raging wolf,
unleashing naked ferocity of life upon life.
Survival reigns supreme.
Tearing pieces of flesh from carcasses
strewn among the ferns and rocks,
wary eyes sweep surrounds.
And so ...
urges prevail as people walk the back alleys
of the megapolis of every continent
seeking satisfactions of depravity
as strains of music along with noise
and the aroma of smoke
float from open doorways and windows,
drifting down causeways.
Such is this thing we call life
in those seldom moments of honest reflection.
How close to the mouth of the cave do we wander?
And why still do we ask,
"From whence springs the softness of seasons
that so inspire
those haunting memories of hope?"

WHERE TO STAND?

Caught on the wave of Manifest Destiny,
swept across a continent,
and sent around the world,
what we did
(for the most part)
was considered admirable.
Except for those times
when the baseness of the soul
captured battered hearts
and left us to our wanton selves.
We are as yet incomplete.
We must learn to
"stand still in silence"
to gain that essential self-perception
from which we direct the soul
to save us.
This will give
that standpoint of maturity that says,
"It all starts with me!"
We must govern for a one to a One
before we implode in our own naiveté.

MEMORIES

"Sundays aren't just Sundays anymore."
Ruminations of a hopeful young man
who used to say
"It looks like rain,"
knowing there'd be no logging
if it rained.
To which the Old Man answered,
"If you wait on the weather
you won't get anything done."
It seemed that if we would just get out there
– into the woods –
being there would drive the clouds away.
It is only now, upon reflection,
that on those few days
when upon arriving at the job site
a sprinkle would come,
I remember he would say,
"Maybe it will let up."
And I was to add,
"Looks like and all-dayer to me."
Little did I know then
that he had an accord with God.
It took those maturing years to realize
just how sincerely he loved woods work.
He's dying now,
and it's raining
– and maybe, they say –
it will be worse this afternoon.
"Damn!"

We had planned a trip to Keith Sidding
and the Swamp Cabin Castle.
Well,
we can have a fire in the fireplace
and play some Cribbage.
We will find something to do
with the Old Man today.
There is one thing we won't do –
wait on the weather.
Years later the disappointment still lingers
about that last woods trip
we didn't get to make.

LIFE AND SCIENCE

The young have a faith in science
that could create opportunities
for the rule of situation ethics.
Employed with a certainty
(used as an oxymoron)
that says,
"Science will exonerate decisions
lacking sufficient ethics in the now."
Justified = further science.
Unjustified = just facts.
It's the journey through the soup that matters.
The superimposition of the sine waves
of being's generations provide
(or should provide)
a "touching" cementing life to life,
or at the very least, confirm life.
Too fast? Too slow?
But life has always had "close enough"
and "the luck of the Irish."
Who is to tell?
Just to have been me,
says it all.

TO SOME OF THE MUSICIANS
OF THE DAY

Music as
synaptic complexity is not consonant
with what has been eternally already there.
Music is not
an eclectic juxtaposition
of dissonance
that opens doors to the loss of integrity.
When I want to be
almost politically correct,
I say,
"You murdering bastards of music,
may God have mercy on your souls,
and may that judgment
come soon."

PERSONHOOD

Our history
distilled in the present's wine,
stimulates different taste buds:
those of the child,
the young, the adolescent,
the maturing young adults,
and finally the maturing old.
Wisdom's won with gifts
of beings' souls.
So ...
Stand in torrents and cyclones!
Know that stillness bathes
each in its time.
Most persons' histories lie buried
in the dust of unknown pasts.
Still,
the visible and somewhat knowable,
all bits and pieces from stupendous effort,
tell tales of their own.
We are remnants weaving paths
from then to now.
Our trails'
signposts tell of waysides
where focus gave reflective pause,
that in assuming sighed,
"Good enough!"
"Bad enough!"
From pedestals of progress,
nourishment flows to souls.

Snacks and sumptuous repasts
nurture Heaven's gifts.
"Better Thans" and "Worse Thans"
adhere to gnomes' mushy spines,
till incidents' choices precipitate
in which blood and life are spent
building bridges
to that infinite self-leading to the Holy of Forever.
How long this trail of human life
from humble fits and starts
to sweeping currents and sublime.
This we know –
the past demands a loving persuasion
always murmuring,
"Yes to life! Yet not all life."[1]
Gifted and haunted
in this Holy Forever,
we live knowing we must know
and knowing we know so little
when voices repeat their whisperings,
"Move slowly on this sacred path."

---

[1] Evil is real. Our challenge is to deal with it. "Justice is mine" sayeth the Lord.
Be patient the Good Book says. And yet, are we not a part of His hand?

PIECES FROM THE NOTE BOOK

The filth and the slime of humanity
are well documented.
In the face of that history,
we can choose to stand and do
what we know is right.
From the cloud of adolescent ignorance,
we can step up to the truth
and in that magnanimous gesture
embrace our holy.
Opportunities to speak of all the
responsibilities to own
the beauty of the truth abound.
We must say yes, or no,
and advance with our deeds
the glory of the present.
Sure we have participated
in the ballet of eternity
and it was our most shining moment.
This is my kind of Christianity,
and my obligation.
The whole swirling mosaic,
broken pieces,
perfectly carved pieces,
edges and centers.
We find it difficult to focus on the whole.
We think we know more than
we can ever see,
giving us a false impression of knowing,
we continue on, thinking we know.
Our pride holds us to a fixed course.
It might lead to a collision
with the truth.

From catharsis to apogee,
a person's life makes a difference.
By leaving tracks for others to follow
we contribute to the great drama of our kind.
When we feel we cannot bear it
we must continue on.
When we see death and destruction,
we must believe and carry on.
To act from within the now
is humankind's greatest challenge.
When we least expect it
and are open to the touch of the Divine,
we feel it,
if we live long enough.
And if we don't,
how many of us die
thinking we have touched the holy?
I will own it as my gift to the present
and to life.
The truth is not what a prelate
deemed right for me,
but what I fought to understand and become.

SOCCER

And finally it happened …
Enough had come,
one way or another,
and they had brought their love with them.
Football,
the real thing,
and they played and they talked about
"their game."
Others listened and wondered.
Meanwhile they played and talked
and then we all started to play too,
big kids, little kids, every kind of kid.
A great gift had been harbored long enough
and was finally shared.
We accepted the gift
and soccer came
to the United States of America.

A NEW SPRING

In this age of
show all – tell all,
we live stirring gruel and porridge.
Looking for self-exposure,
egos hang on willow wands
bobbing in the wind.

THE CU CU RU CU CU

Like the cu cu ru cu cu of the mourning dove
touches the seared edges of souls
wanting to be felt by lost love,
we listen to the strains of
life and wonder why.

THE OLD WALL

The sides of a house, the walls,
stood for centuries,
or for decades.
What have they heard and felt –
scuffings, scrapings, tappings,
touchings,
heat, cold?
A young child walked by the ruins and said,
"What was that old wall for?"
I sighed and answered,
"It held the lives of many.
Now it feeds our dreams."

THE U.N.

A skirmish here,
a clash there,
a power struggle here,
a little ethnic cleansing there.
Madness rears its ugly head,
and finally,
for the first time we have
the means to restrain it.
Where's the integrity,
the courage?[1]

---

[1] The earth is almost round, and in those protuberances and vales, we witness the corruption of our kind.

WARRIOR'S LAMENT

In defense of life,
I'm killing you.
You didn't listen when it was said,
"Life is sacred."
I'm killing you
because you murdered another child.
If you murdered one, you deserve to die.
I'm killing you
before you rape another maiden.
If you raped one, you deserve to die.
I'm killing you
before you slaughter other elders
in the marketplace.
If you slaughtered one, you deserve to die.
I'm killing you
before you sacrifice more worshipers
as they go about their daily prayers.
If you sacrificed one, you deserve to die.
In defense of life,
I'm killing you.
You didn't listen when it was said,
"Life is sacred."

WHAT AM I?

I touch the earth.
I touch the sky.
And still I wonder why
in touching both
I touch myself.
Am I some of both,
or all the same?
And if I am,
who's to blame for magic moments
set aflame
of tortured memories of
the game?

WHAT ARE YOU THIKING?

Just ramblings.
Behind the curve, ahead of the curve,
I do not know.
I'm too busy keeping my eye on the ball.
How much I wish I was
wearing out a stirrup.
Memories of the freshness of outdoors
give way to the smell of oldness.
Scenes flash through the mind.
Intent takes knowledge.
How do we know?
And how should we be judged
if we don't know?
We must protect a child long enough
for them to learn "really me."

WHAT DO WE DO?

The tit for tat of politics
runs the gamut of sublime to grotesque.
Yet ...
A few lives – more or less,
always make a difference,
feeding the monsters and the angels.
When history turns away from courage
because of fear,
what is left?
My presence exudes an
"I'm here how!"
I walk by a stranger
and nod with a smile.
Yet ...
They don't even look up,
there is no acknowledgment of any kind.
Who knows what weight they carry
on this magnificent Fall day?
In any case it appears they are not here.
What do we do when we are here
and everyone else is someplace else?

STRIKE FORCE

More than just enough,
less than too much,
life threads the needle of the possible.
From a democracy of biology and our own kind
rings a message:
"All *men* are created equal"
and *still* "we are engaged in a Great Civil War
testing whether *that nation*, or *any nation* so conceived
and so dedicated
can long endure."
On the altars of our battlefields the value of the species
becomes a holy sacrifice.
The rational animal's personal integrity encompasses
a universal commitment to life:
A life which begets and fosters more life,
and yet, not all life.
The cancers of our now and future,
many the gifts of progress and numbers,
are set to assail the soft tissue of fellow travelers.
We ride on a spaceship
that is not responsible for its privileged inhabitants.
Therefore
we must develop a resolve:
Surgery is a must.
Cancers must be removed.
Healthy flesh
will be invaded and infringed upon.
The living paradox: Yes/No.
Life's mandate: Some yes/All no,
Enough of everything/Not too much of anything.
The mystical demands participation
in the paradox of the existential totality.

The execution of our presence can only be done
with the law of love.
In seeking the Truth of the Now
we must get close enough
to the edge of God's mind
without losing sight of our souls.
Our challenge is to train soldiers for surgical strikes,
while attuning minds of citizens
to know when to send them into theaters of operation,
and to support them while they are there
and to welcome them home when they are done.
Existence is *educere*,
the leading out of complex Truths
from within,
Now!
and without,
Now!
All becoming in the present.
Unless we choose to maintain a commitment
to excise the insidious malevolence
of our brothers and our sisters,
we will not be able to exert control and deterrence
at the heart and periphery of our kind.
Freedom and restraint lie in the balance:
Close enough! Swift enough!
Now![1]

---

[1] "Strike Force" first appeared in *Always Extolling, A Collection* (2005).

WIND SWEPT

Swirling dust sweeps across the land
down adobe-lined streets
where amidst the tumult
sloped and hunched shoulders
hide from the onslaught
of an early spring in a desolate desert.
Yet
there is always life
coming and going, like the dust,
like the strains of an eternal flute,
¡El bogo va![1]
is heard in the howling wind.
And as counterpoint
we hear echoes of that
crescendoing Maslowian,
"No!"
It breaks across the pandemic
of insipid human efforts
and jolts a sufficient number of hearts and minds,
giving them enough energy of focus
to enable new births.
Birth that reaches up and out
meeting with all the other efforts,
coming alive from above,
below, and within.

---

[1] "The boat is leaving!" That haunting cry from the novel Doña Bárbara.

WOLF'S TRIFLINGS

From a small cabin window,
I peek out at the shaking pines
tossed by the mighty hands of the wind.
Early Spring days, reminiscent of Fall,
present gray clouds that dull the day.
The mind grinds away
seeking the smithy's forge
where light and heat,
wrought with commitment,
form new solutions
to the daily reflections on global politics.
All seeming so petty,
yet so unmanageable.
And then,
I look out another window and find
iris basking in the afterglow
of the wolf's triflings.

WORDS

When crashing pixilated abstractions,
accompanied by bombastic explosions,
assault eyes and ears,
we turn to words.
Minds struggle in transition.
In some heroic attempt at understanding,
we swim in vast seas of pollinated forms
reminding us of the overlays of reality.
Spiked balls of touching tentacles
stretching into space,
much like information bits,
are cast amongst our fathomings.
An "I" lingers
isolated from the center
of a liquid flowing of mechanics
that spreads the process of life maintenance,
intergalactic interactions of bio and astrophysics
we call them.
While in rampant succession
rural and urban nuclei burst
in powerful expressions
casting seeds
to raging winds and torrents
creating new life forms
needing love.
And all this lies
in the firmament of words.

A BORDER

To stand and peer through a fence
at a large house and a beautiful yard
invokes dreams of things to have,
things to do.
To look across a river,
a line in the sand, a road,
at another country
wishing, wondering, hoping, fearing
the possibilities of new things,
seeking opportunities,
wanting adventures,
looking for new places, cold places with snow,
finding others who speak the language
of tortillas and tortas, chiles and cajeta.
I am filled with a mixture of
excitement and apprehension –
both elixirs of life.
To live for new and betterments
of life has always been the purpose of life.
When will the world awaken to the new responsibilities
of the twenty-first century?
Will it only be when everyone understands
we all followed the same path,
are on the same path?

BEGGING GOD

"One more word!"
"Ah …"
"One more phrase!"
"Uh …"
"One more sentence!"
"Mum …"
"One more paragraph!"
"Humph …"
"One more page!"
"Ah ha …"
"One more chapter!"
"Um um …"
"One more book!"
"Cupiditas! Cupiditas!
All rivers of life run into the sea of the dead."
"So …?"
"One more word that becomes flesh
is all I will allow.
Go forth!
Do good things!"

BOOKS

Wanderers,
throughout the cresting waves of time
and shifting sands of change,
to you who carried books in trunks,
chests, knapsacks, saddlebags,
and pockets,
I bless your efforts.

FALSE PRIDE

As they fled in their moment of panic
he said,
"Do you love me?"
Then,
concerned for their safety,
he turned his attention to the raging crowd.
She answered,
"With my whole heart!
My love!"
He didn't hear her words.
For hours they fought their way
through the tangled mass of humanity.
Then …
heaving breathless and sweating
they paused.
He wondered,
"Does she love me?
She wondered,
"Did he hear me?"

* * *

Years after their separation,
having both taken different paths,
they found each other
as they sat on a park bench
soaking in the last crimson rays
of the setting sun.
Turning towards what he thought
was a stranger,
He said,
"I loved a person once."
She answered,
"I did too."

In a thunderbolt of recognition
they both said,
"Are you …"
"Yes!"
He said,
"Why didn't you answer me when I asked you
if you loved me?"
"I did. Why didn't you hear me?
"I thought you didn't say anything."
"I thought you heard me and didn't care."
"Why didn't you tell me again?"
"Why didn't you ask me again?"
"I had asked you once
from the depths of my heart."
"I answered you once
from the depths of my soul."
"But I didn't hear you."
"You didn't ask again."
Suddenly tears poured from sunken eyes.
Two souls snared in the clutches of false pride
had refused to be honest with their
most profound need to know.
Both had let the thought of thinking they knew
rob them of a lifetime of sharing their love.
"Why didn't you ask again,"
she said weepingly.
"Why didn't you repeat what you said?"
he begged with sodden eyes.

Foolish hesitations have crushed
naïve and stubborn souls
for eons.
The time has come to be honest
with what we feel
and with what we want to know.
"I love you!"
must be said again and again,
in an embrace
as lips touch and eyes meet.
In a touching attention
we are bound to our truths
as we share ourselves with each other.

* * *

They fell wracked with weeping
into each other's arms
touching for the first time the depths of truths
long carried in broken near-empty vessels.
The sin of false pride
had stolen years of boundless joy.

FROM TROUBLED DREAMS AWAKENED

August doldrums seep into
an overworked, underfed,
foggy memory bank.
A realization boils.
Mist rises.
Like a jagged tipped iceberg,
most of it below the surface,
the dawning of awareness
slams me against the wall of the present.
What is happening to the culture of my world?
Baseball is out.
Soccer is in.
Where in this cyclone of change am I?
A nanosecond's reflection shouts,
"What is your stand?"
What do I stand for?
Where do I stand on anything?
Do I stand for anything?
Am I currently and actively
intending to be anything at all?
Do I have to answer questions
about baseball and soccer
before I begin to get closer
to understanding my question?
Well ... Yes I do!
comes as a sledgehammer
smashing into my workplace.
Where has the robust figure of the umpire gone,
the one who boomed,
in those latter days of May,
"Play ball!"

The one whose presence
spoke volumes of the intrigue
and intricacies of a new culture,
that amalgam of the "Old World,"
that melting pot of the "New World"?
Where has the essence of the player's soul gone?
Into what kind of person have we devolved
so as to lose the sacredness
of a national pastime?
No!
Not true!
We now have the NFL!
The Super Bowl and all that.
No!
Wait a minute!
Now it is soccer and The World Cup.
Weeknights and weekends
are full of tiny tots of all kinds
stumbling and running
adoring their flying little feet,
forgetting there is a ball on the field somewhere,
a goal to be made, reached, or scored.
Perhaps it is …
that in the sanctity of growth
we have exploded with the illumination
of knowing
we are all just children.
That must be it,
or how else could we explain
the wanton disregard for others of our own kind
and the world at large
lurking in such a gigantic pool of generosity?
We appear as little children,
running and jumping with the sheer joy of life.

Yet some are lost from that maturing reflection that says,
"Don't break it!
It, all of it, has a life of its own."
There are those who seem to have escaped
that bathing warmth of wisdom:
We are a part of a whole.
We owe something precious to each one
and everything.
The physicists of the day say,
"If we touch at all, we touch the all,
and sometimes the All."
A striking circumstance presents itself
clamoring in a loud voice,
"Where is the reverence
of and for those ancient times,
with a sacred wonder of it all?"
And then the biophysicists join in and say,
"It's all biophysics!"
Like that is supposed to tell us how to pray,
how to know that love matters
and that we must tread gently
on the gifts of the present.
How is it that we have allowed spiked hair,
held in place with goop,
to depict the unkempt,
and bagging pants that force a swagger
that bends our bones,
and noises and explosions of light
that pass for art and music,
to assault the senses
of the living soul?
On this,
I brood in the early morning's light.

* * *

Then,
glancing out the window to reassure myself,
I see a perched dragonfly
drying new wings
and a tiger-striped butterfly
battering at my window.
And I,
I spend my time worrying about such triflings.
Caught in the metamorphosis of all life,
my cultural blinders have,
again,
inhibited my understanding of the whole.

GARBAGE OF THE MIND

Some graffiti and some Internet content
have commonalities.
Much is just garbage to the eye and mind.
When neophytes offer advice
it must be sifted and winnowed
with wisdom of the ages.
When political parties write on walls
they send messages that conflict
aesthetically with government.
Speaking in splashes
of color and nonsense
they offer less than prudence.
If form dictates content,
as the astrophysicists say,
trash on walls,
or screens
can't have too much to say –
except that idiots abound.
Desecration of the communal,
shouts in foul language
to senseless souls
who already know less than enough.

HANDS ON!

Do it now!
Touch!
Caress!
Listen!
Living with the word turned flesh
is an absolute.
When there is a living dialog
we are touching.
Admonition:
Those lost in the existential smoke and mirrors
of our current confusion,
those panting and out of breath,
stop and take the extended
hand of truth.
There is an ocean of difference between
healthy skepticism
and the deception of paranoia.

TO DREAM[1]

"La vida es sueño y los sueños, sueños son."
(Life is a dream, and dreams are only dreams.)[2]

I dreamt about a new skin/membrane,
a multipurpose-universal,
internal-external,
concept-fabric
that is intrinsically interactive
– protective – open.
A responsive, living
(and I know that is redundant)
holographicness,
that is *efeta* stuff,
where IT–WE
is always becoming I–WE
and love-life prevails.

---

[1] This is to remind us, again. This poem first appeared in *Sign Posts, Volume V*.
I think it bears repeating.
[2] *La Vida es Sueño - Segismundo*, by Pedro Calderón de la Barca.

IN THE FACE OF FEAR

Every age has had its choices
– run, hide, submit, succumb,
and even expire,
or stand tall, be creative, courageous,
meet the challenge;
choose life!
The truth of the human presence
provides a history of surmounting mountain tops
and being swept away in valleys.
There has always been a relationship
between life and death.
In the face of this,
we have proven to be resilient.
We have,
in the face of war,
natural disasters, and pestilence,
survived.
More of us have more and are able to do more
than ever before in the history of the species.
This seems to fly in the face
of the daily myopic media coverage
of the human story.
(This by no means belittles
the wonderful programs
of archaeology, natural history, and daily heroics.)
Fear's immobilizing ugly face
has never gained the upper hand.

There have been those moments
of doubt
and the wonder about death that formed
the background of an omnipresent feature
of the human portrait.
Yet it is to the foreground,
"that which is yet to come"
upon which we have fixed our gaze
that has enabled us to continue
to manifest our sense of
"I am!"
in the face of fear.
Adverse human circumstances
have provided opportunities
for celebration and reflection
– and more reflection and celebration.
One could say,
we are the dancing, singing, pondering species.
It is in the joy and exuberance of life,
as well as the studious,
create it, fix it, change it attitude,
that we have always said
a resounding yes to life!
There has always been a preponderance
of faith, hope, and love.
The innate drive to awareness
of the presence of the person is –
yes we can and yes we will.

MONDAY
(MARCH 3, 2008)

On the heels of a terrorist leader's death
troops mass on borders.
Students march on the U.S. embassy
in Moscow, protesting policies.
U.S. air strikes hit Al Qaeda in Somalia.
Rockets launched from Gaza
fall on Israel.
Troops withdraw,
preparing for new incursions.
The U.N. passes another sanction
against Iran's nuclear program.
Eco terrorists strike
in a suburb of Seattle.
More tornados roar through tornado alley.
Planes land without landing gear.
Power passes and stays the same
in corrupt elections in Russia.
Lawyers protest the government
in Islamabad.
A magnitude 7 earthquake strikes
islands in the pacific.
First presidential visit happens between
the new Iraq and Iran.
Terrorists are arrested in Saudi Arabia.
The Taliban attack NATO headquarters
in southern Afghanistan.
A teenager murders his mother
and two sisters.
Seven shot inside Wendy's.
And myriad other "happenings"
occurred that I know not of,
reported and not.

86

Most, of course,
were of an incredible variety of
an abundance of absolutely
wonderful things,
every second, of every minute,
of every hour, of every day.
Tuesday
will bring more of the same.

IT TAKES TWO

Does it take a dialog to set the record straight?
Yes it does!
To enter and to become one with,
is the holy human grail.
Blessed we are and blessed we must become.
It is from that sacred triumvirate of
Thought, Word, and Deed
that we take our roles and parse communion
to and with all others.
When do we become aware
of the holy undertaking?
It is always in those silent inner sanctums
of the self that we are given to realizations
of yeses and nos.
The paths are many yet the way is narrow.
In the end there is forever only one of us
with whom we learn that sacred dance,
have that inner struggle,
win the Great Battle.
Hearken to those troubling moments
when we must choose to capture
flights of the mind,
those that mirror the Divine Will.
As truth floats across the necessary of our understanding,
stand still and reflect.
Grab that spiral helix of His and Mine
and holding on to both
become that bond
that makes the real stay its course.

PATTY SAYS ...

Patty says,
"What does the Diddler do?"
Restoration of Being's focus
in the Process of Becoming.
He first heals the person from
a variety of wounds:
childhood trauma,
absence of love,
physical and emotional abuse,
death,
adult trauma,
relationships,
confusion.
After the person understands the wounds
they open windows and doors
and light shines in.
Healing begins.
The person then is put on the path of
"Seeing"
the real self and the world.
The consciousness of truth is awakened
and union of the self with
God, nature, and people established.
Once this is in place
the person can begin to grow
in the light of the truth of the now
and become who they really are.
This is what the Diddler does.

PATH TO THE SELF

From eons of our efforts
come tracks of human kind.
Each and every one,
from the dawn of time,
when we realized a self,
had within us and before us a trail.
A longing and a belonging was engendered.
We are all now and have forever been
pulled and pushed.
"Take the reins of ourselves!"
always our greatest challenge.
To be! Go forthright
into our days and our tomorrows!
Live well! Love! Die well!
From consternations of our choices,
we labored with the options.
We have the commandments of the ages,
to every culture and every time
there have been those gates and walls.
What we need are universal truths
for mastering the craft
of being with our kind.
Strewn amidst those eons,
rules raised their friendly hands,
and grasping wayward souls
led them to their path.[1]

---

[1] See "The Rules" *from The Game of Life: A Player's Manual For Executives And Others*, by Don Davison.

THE CROSSING

I was standing in the living room of my parents' nearly empty house, gazing out over the storm-tossed waves of Lake Lucerne. The wind was out of the northwest – the back side of the front was passing slowly. Stalled for the moment, or so I thought.

Suddenly there was a pounding on the back door. Pulled from my memories of being a teenager when we used to take the canoe out in storms such as this to "test the mettle of the man" in our naïve adolescent bravado, I walked to the back door to find the guests who were staying in the neighbor's cabin.

Opening the screen door I said nonchalantly, "Come in out of the storm." Two people hurriedly came in and turned, both talking excitedly, "There is a real bad problem over at Water's Edge (a resort directly across the lake). Five people have been critically injured and one presumed dead in a very bad auto accident. The road is shut down and there is no power at all around the lake. The EMT squad wants to know if anyone can go and help out." I asked, "Aren't the EMTs available?" They began to explain, "No, not a single team from Crandon, Argonne, or Wabeno is available. There are critically injured people all along the path of a freak tornado that passed through as part of the storm, and they have all been dispatched to various sites. They heard that there was a doctor in the house here."

My mind flew into a mental retort, *Yeah! A PhD in Philosophical and Social Foundations! That won't fit the bill.* They had only heard the Dr. part and in any case didn't know who I was. It had been too many years since I had left my natal surrounds, a small town, the lake, and Timber

Ranch. My brief return visits had, for the most part, gone unnoticed. There had been no time to "catch up" with the few who may still remember a fellow Crandonite. My parents' home was seven miles out of town on the east shore of beautiful Lake Lucerne and I had been gone for many, many years.

Suddenly, flashing through my mind came images of broken bones, severe lacerations, internal injuries, and the fact that it was a four-mile trip either way around the lake to get there with a storm that had blocked the road in many places with downed trees, power lines, and branches. The roads were impassable. Life hung in the balance and I thought, *I should go see what I can do to help.*

My mind returned to the present and I thanked them for the news and said, "I will go!" Such a simple answer given without realizing that I had to cross a mile of windswept lake with two-foot waves bearing down from almost the opposite direction. My mind was still caught in the foolish episodes of my youth when, if the canoe would capsize, we would just right it and keep on "testing the wind and waves."

A shadow crossed my mind and a realization presented itself: *I am 75 years old and not the same person – except in that "can do" attitude that has served me marvelously well over all those intervening years.*

My thoughts returned to the immediate problem: They would have all the medical supplies at the resort. All I could offer was a willing person and a pair of hands. I was that on both accounts. I quickly threw my raincoat on and headed down to the shore. The waves were pounding incessantly. This was early spring and the only mode of transportation was a canoe. Could I even get it in the water? Braving the winds, I dragged the canoe down to the dock and with the waves rocking the dock and sloshing over I managed to get it far enough out to slide it into water on the lee side of the dock and gingerly stepped in. Dropping to my knees in the bottom just ahead of the back seat in order to keep my weight low and somewhat centered in the canoe, I shoved off with my paddle.

Immediately the huge waves carried me clear of the dock and I started paddling southwest. I knew I would have to make corrections along the way in order to end up straight across the lake. And even if I did drift too far to the southwest I could come back to the resort in the lee of the shore on the west side of the lake. Or, if necessary, beach the canoe and walk to the resort. That was the plan. I plunged my paddle into the raging tempest and started across the lake.

In good weather it would be a trip of twenty-five to thirty minutes to make the crossing. This trip's duration would be an open question. In my mind came the thought, *Stay slightly southwest and take advantage of every trough to swing straight west.* The roiling waves continuously rocked the canoe as the rhythm of dipping my paddle and pulling hard with a slight twist as the righting of the course set in. For a time the task brought me back to those glorious battles of my youth and I reveled in those memories and the sheer joy of freedom and effort. It was exhilarating. I pressed on.

The reverie was short lived. I was not the same powerful youth of my yesteryears. The exertion of old muscles quickly began to take their toll. "Slow down! Slow and steady will get the job done," I said out loud. The same words used by my father when he saw his young sons rushing through the logging tasks. We were always hell-bent precisely on getting the job done and getting back to the water and the lake.

Summers were spent getting up at four in the morning to hit the woods by five. We knew that by two in the afternoon, one of us would be in the runabout and the other on a slalom ski, weaving our way up and down just off the shoreline. At times we'd be jumping over branches and trees that had tumbled into the lake, frolicking with friends in paradise. Thinking back on those times let me slip into a state of delicious remembrance, of beautiful long days of endless fun, albeit interspersed with those never-ending adolescent wonderings: *Would things go well on the water? What about the beach party tonight? Who will sit next to me?* But the omnipresent task of the now lay in an ever-present relentless battering of rain, waves, and buffetings of the wind.

Slowly, the realization began to sink in. My rational mind owned the reality of the seriousness of an accident – and yet my mind also began to own the seriousness of my impending journey. The facts of the matter were that I had made, more impulsively than consciously, a promise that I would go when I was told they needed assistance. My mind recalled the conversation with the guests at the house. They mentioned a "Dr. in the house." Well, while that was technically true, the Dr. "business" was a PhD. Not exactly the person you would call for a medical emergency. Nevertheless, I had accepted the challenge of the offer to provide whatever assistance I could. That I was game to offer any help I could, had always been my style, and now, with the daunting task of each deep stroke of the paddle and each twisting push to correct the direction of my crossing, I was on my way in a commitment to my "new now." In slowing, I began to release my mind from my body and the physicality of its efforts and entered into a world of my thoughts. The word "style," what kind of a word was that?

What a word for those crisscrossing currents of thoughts, actions, and efforts that comprise a human life.

The irony presented itself with a rush. As if it could be that adjectives really defined a loving, breathing being with an independent mind. The word *style* was defined by the dictionary as *Stylus*, writing tool (I knew something of that), a manner similar to another writer of literary form (I knew something about that too). Fashion as an acceptable mode of behavior or dress; elegance, fashionable. (I knew little and cared less about that.)

How was it that my mind had picked that word *style* to describe my life? Character mattered, but style? Had I somehow along the way of life been seduced into thinking I was immune to the language of the day, to the cares and druthers of others, a public that really knew next to nothing about the others that surrounded them. They were, in my limited opinion, too self-centered, too adolescent. Ah ha! Was I caught in my current circumstance reliving some subconscious realization that in those fun-loving busy days of my youth I cared too little? Was I caught in the "showing off" of my prowess on the water, skiing with anything, including canoe paddles, and no skis at all, just bare-foot across the water?

A doubt had crept in and demanded its measure of attention with which I was to contend in my semiconscious wanderings and wonderings. As my physical body kept up its relentless pace and my musing seemed to be a detached form of entertainment, my mind turned to the long list of choices that we make from child to adolescent, from adolescent to maturing young adult, and finally to the seemingly never-ending ripening years of a maturing adult. There was always a mish-mash of those accumulations of

95

new and old points of departure when faced with new circumstances, new challenges.

Now, as my body had warmed to my current efforts and the good habits of my youthful days, a rhythm returned to old muscles, and I continued to reminisce about the long road of choices and commitments that had provided moments of ecstasies and sorrows, accomplishments and failures.

As my body kept up its methodical movements, my mind slowly became consciously aware of a receding shoreline. I was making progress and I was maintaining a good heading.

Then, as if by some switch, my mind was again passing through my life's journey. I had moved from smart athlete to interested learner, even admirer of the great works of literature, those filled with stellar words of wisdom, wisdom that I had learned to share with students, those in my counseling practice, and others; words that I was convinced would produce those incremental flashes of insight that could help, if commitment was maintained, a wayward soul. I had indeed used the word *sojourn* often over the years. It became a trademark of my writing, my counseling, and my teaching.

Suddenly, my train of thought was interrupted by a sharp pain, and then a persistent aching in my arms and hands. The dipping of the paddle, the pulling hard through the water, the twisting of the paddle to adjust for drift, they were all beginning to catch up to me.

Then, as with all new awarenesses, my mind began to own the seriousness of my current moment in the stream of the present. (All bodies are in motion.) Through the driving downpour I could see that I was nearing the middle of the lake and was now exposed to the full force of the elements. There had been a time or two when the canoe had rolled almost to the tipping point. I had shifted my weight and used my paddle to stabilize the canoe – but now, now as the fatigue of the journey was setting in, I began to realize that should I capsize it would be nearly impossible to "right the ship."

A new level of focus and intent began to grow in my mind. A short review of my journey so far, the physical and mental woofing and weaving of my activities and the realization that I was only halfway to my destination had finally made a fundamental impression on my mind: If I was to survive this trip, if I was to make good on my intentions to offer some form of acceptable assistance, I had better get down to the business of everything I had to contend with. I had to come to grips with a "mantra moment" that would concentrate my efforts and my intentions. I was alone in the middle of a storm in the middle of a reasonably large lake, in a rather large – well okay, a really large storm. The predictions had been that it would be a slow-moving storm lasting several days. The Nordic winds had passed but the high winds and rain were projected to last for a day or two.

I had to be efficient. I had to concentrate on the tasks at hand. My willingness to go, the suddenness of my leaving to offer help, and what now had become a personal struggle to care for myself, were all to be integrated, "prioritized," as the lingo of the day was so oft to say, in spite of the fact that we many times do not have enough information at hand to even begin the process of weighing and measuring the dross from the treasure.

The facts were obvious: the storm, the wind, the rain, the waves, the canoe, and me, a shore a half-mile away, injuries needing attention, time was of the essence.

A mantra began to form in my mind and to direct my body: me, focus, true, mine, now, and that distillation of the past, "love thy neighbors as thyself." My "I" became a "me" as tasks of self-ownership and purpose, always in the context of the eternal now, were forever lying out before me. These were the fundamentals I lauded in The Rules in my seminal academic work, *The Game of Life – A Player's Manual for Executives and Others*.[1] I had used them for decades in my classes, my counseling, and my writing. They had come originally as a reflective coalescence while thinking about efficient ways to get people to know enough, to focus enough, to care enough and to respect enough, and finally, to be able to believe enough to make their life happen in responsible ways, ways that were always life affirming. Always participating in that great process of complementing life as it is, always is, and always will be: a self-coincidental exercise in shared being as an integral part of the whole.

In my heart I had owned those Rules as the primordial points of departure for every living person. Now, my very own life would depend upon my exuding an integrity of being for myself and for others.

---

[1] The Game has 5 cards, 7 rules, and 5 corollaries. The rules for children are explained in depth while being exactly the same for adults. (Children just have fewer cards to play.) The sameness of The Rules is a feature very much appreciated by parents as well as children. That there are rules came as a new realization for many. The explanation for children is enlightening in that many parents have said, "I enjoyed so much reading The Rules for Children. They put it all in context for me." (http://amzn.to/fOrqEi)

My back from my neck on down burned like wildfire. My aching hands and arms were like lead and there was only water, wind, and time. I repeated the mantra: "Me, focus, true, mine, now, love, holiness reigns." And then again: "Me, focus, true, mine, now, love, holiness reigns," words that embodied the very heart of the seven rules for the *Game of Life*.

I saw only the moving surface of the roiling water and that was all. Time seemed to stand still. Nothing seemed to change. The paddle went up and down and turned, up, back, down, turned. Over and over again, I became an "it" moving towards itself in a vast tumultuous sea of wind, rain, and waves, intoning a mantra that I believed, that I lived, that I had shared so many times with so many. I was now an embodiment of the truths as I had presented them so many times in so many ways. My very life was now dependent on what I would choose to do.

Then, in that omnipresent halo of self-perception and self-preservation, that melding into one, I realized I was coming up to the shore. I had made it across the lake. As the canoe slid along the gravel up to the waterline I knelt up and slowly put my cramped legs and feet over the wale into the shallow cold water. It was a refreshing feeling in the spring-fed lake. The water was a gift from the depths far below. I straightened myself up and looked across the shoreline and there to my surprise was the resort barely 200 yards away.

Still ensconced in my mantra focus, I beached the canoe and moved quickly towards the crowd surrounding the main building of the resort. Some people turned and asked, "Are you the Dr. from across the lake?" I nodded and added, "Not exactly what you expected, but I'm here to help if I can."

Grabbing me by the hand they led me to the dining room where five people were laid out on tables. All were badly hurt but in good hands. Not thinking of the consequences, I blurted out, "I thought there were six." Silence reigned. Finally, the owner of the resort came over and said in a low voice, "We had to leave him where he was. We couldn't get to him. We think he is dead."

I immediately turned and glancing over the crowd, saw a young man who looked capable, and asked, "Can you take me there?" Nodding, he said, "Sure!" And then he bolted for the door. I followed. He jumped on a four-wheeler and I mounted on behind. He switched on the ignition, the motor caught, and with throttle roaring we headed up the hill to the main road and turned north. He said the accident was about half a mile down the road. We proceeded to weave our way around downed power lines, broken branches, and trunks of trees. Litter was everywhere. We exchanged names and he told me he had gone home, he lived right across the road from the resort, and got his four-wheeler and had helped with the retrieval of the other victims.

Suddenly, we came upon a large white pine that had toppled over across the road. He stopped the four-wheeler, jumped off, and ran down into the ditch and up to the edge of the woods. There, in the most smashed and mangled condition, the car was resting right side up with the front against a huge aspen. It had rolled over what appeared to be several times on its way down and up to its final resting place.

I followed Jimmy (we had exchanged names on the way to the accident) to the car and immediately knelt down. Peering under the car's smashed-in top, I saw only a little bit of a person's arm. I stretched to see more but most of the console had been broken loose at an angle and covered the body.

I ran around to the other side. I could barely see through the small opening of the window and the crumpled door. All that was visible were two feet with what appeared to be new shoes. I caught my classifying mind and reprimanded myself, "Stay focused!" I turned to the crumpled hood and realized it had bent and rolled up in the rolling over and the smashing against the rocks and trees. I quickly assessed the situation and thought if we had some tools we might be able to pull the hood up enough to get a chain or cable down to the console and move it back far enough to get a better idea of the condition of the body. I told Jimmy if he could get a couple of winches and a crow bar we might be able to do something. He nodded and said, "Not a problem! I have my logging tools in the back of my truck, I'll be right back." Then, he was off like a rocket.

In the meantime, in the semi-protection of the forested edge of the road, through the wind and rain, I surveyed the car again. It was totally demolished. I approached the side of the car and stretched my arm out. I found myself thinking, "It's hard to think anyone could have survived." I knelt beside the right side of the car, putting my arm down through the smashed-out window, trying to touch the ankle of the man inside. I could hardly reach that far but I found that by placing my whole body forward along the crumpled fender I could almost touch his left ankle. I stretched with every ounce of energy I could muster and could just barley touch the ankle with the tip of my middle finger. Pressing as hard as I could I was barely able to maintain contact. I gritted my teeth and gave all I had to the effort of holding my finger on the ankle. I waited. My labored breathing slowed. I continued to stretch and hold still trying to calm every part of my body.

"Me, focus, true, mine, now, with love there is always hope."
I repeated over and over again the mantra of my crossing,
attempting to sense anything that would hint of a heartbeat.
I continued to stretch and hold still trying to calm every part
of my body. "Nothing, there is nothing!" I thought. With-
drawing my arm, I took several deep breaths and repeated
my movements stretching again as far as I could. Then, I
thought, "Yes! I think I feel a slow but rhythmic almost
imperceptible throbbing!" I concentrated my attention. I
touched the ankle again and held on, stretching and sensing
with my whole being, waiting for the straining to dissipate
and leave my sense of touch to itself. "There it was again, a
pulse!" I felt the slow but consistent throbbing. I was sure he
was alive. Suddenly, Jimmy came bounding down and up
over the ditch with some tools, two winches, several skid-
ding chains, an axe, and a cant-hook.

I said, "I think he is alive. Let's see what we can do." I stood
up and surveyed the scene again. The large aspen seemed to
be the only purchase point strong enough for the winches. I
quickly explained what I thought would be our best plan of
action. We fastened the cable of the winch some seven feet
up on the trunk and then wrapping a chain around the
crumpled corners of the hood we both started to ratchet it up.
Once tight, we slowly began the methodical movements of
raising it up. There was a screeching tearing sound as the
hood started to give way. Slowly it rose up enough to get the
cant-hook under the edge of the console behind the broken
front of the console panel. We then put our weight down on
the handle. The console moved ever so slightly. We
repositioned the cant-hook and continued to push down until
we heard a snapping "Pop!" The remaining bolts on the
panel held. We found a short piece of log and placed it under
the hood to hold it in place. I told Jimmy to take the second
winch and hook it to the inside edge of the hood near where

the hood hinge was located and to attach the winch to a balsam not very far away from the car on the other side. He hooked it up and we tightened the cable. While he cranked the winch I lifted up on the cant-hook again. The console continued to move. We then secured the hood again by shoving the short piece of log further into the opening of the hood.

I knelt down and checked the panel in back of the motor. It was bent but not broken or cracked. "Good news, bad news, who knows?" The old Chinese saying flitted through my mind. I quickly said to myself, "Slow down!" We checked the winch on the large aspen and found it was slack so we brought the chain around and hooked it to a corner of the console and the heater intake on the panel. Then we again both slowly started cranking on the handle of the winch. It kept bending and I thought this is one time when I hope the rivets won't hold. There was a snap and as we continued another one snapped. The corner of the panel had lifted just enough to form a triangular hole through to the inside. I could now see the man's near-side leg up to the thigh. I bent down and hunted for the artery. Relaxing my breathing and concentrating on my fingers, I felt a stronger heartbeat.

I stepped back and looked at the smashed top and door, which was crushed horizontally to the body of the car. No way out through the doors, there just seemed to be no way to move the collapsed console back far enough to create enough space to let the whole body, part of which was under the steering column, get free enough so that we could slide him out from under the console and through the opening where the console had been pulled back. I walked around to the rear of the car, and thinking out loud said, "We could attached the winch from the aspen to the rear bumper mounts and slip a cable through the opening where the rear window had been and see if we could get the cable around the console and pull it away from the body." Jimmy nodded and brought the winch around from the front of the car. The log would hold the hood up and the other winch would continue to secure the front panel. We attached the hook of the winch to the rear bumper support and put the hook of the cable through the opening of the rear window. We could only get it in for the length of an arm. I said, "Just a moment!" I went to the tool box and grabbed the axe and turning away from the car towards the woods I looked for a strong but slender maple. One that had a good branch that when cut and trimmed would serve as an excellent hook. I did the necessary trimming and walked back to the rear window opening and began to slide the sapling though to the triangular hole in the front panel. Jimmy hooked the cable to the sapling and I slowly pulled the cable through over the seats all the way past the console to the triangular opening. Jimmy smiled and said, "Good thinking!" The cable had followed along nicely and when I hooked it around the console Jimmy's face broke into a grin. I said, "Not so fast! We still have to pull the console back away from the body, and then, hopefully, we can remove him by sliding him through the opening out along the motor."

With little difficulty, we slowly winched the console back far enough to, little by little, slip the injured driver out of the car. Thank God the body was turned sideways and we could gently bend his legs which seemed to be in good shape and slowly pull him out. We had no way of knowing how serious his injuries were and so we took all the prudent cautions. We could only pray we were not adding to the problems. The words *slow and steady* echoed in my mind.

Finally, we had the body out and lying on the cold wet ground. I told Jimmy to cut two ten-foot saplings heavy enough to carry him. He jumped right to the task as I stripped my jacket and zipped it up. Jimmy saw what I had done, stopped and shucked his coat and continued after the saplings. I also zipped his up. Jimmy finished dressing up the saplings and we then slipped both coats up through the arms over the two saplings and we both said, "That will do!"

We gently placed the injured man on our makeshift travois and slid it up to the road. Lashing it to the tool box on the four-wheeler, we slowly towed it back to the resort. When we arrived we saw three ambulances in the parking lot. I asked where they were from. Someone said two came from Monico and one from Elcho. I asked how they got the news. They said they had been monitoring the chatter on the waves 24/7 and because the storm had moved through their area it was no longer a threat so they had responded. Three EMT teams and three ambulances. "Perfect for the job!" I thought. A crowd had gathered when they saw us coming and they rushed over to see who was on the stretcher. There was a little girl with them, one of the accident victims, with her broken arm in a sling and bandages on her head and hands. She walked up to the travois and kneeled down, saying, "Daddy, are you going to be okay?" I stepped up and put my hand on her shoulder. I said, "He can't talk just now. But the EMTs will take care of him."

The EMTs swiftly placed him on the gurney and rolled him into the ambulance. In the blink of an eye all the victims of the accident were gone up the hill and down the highway. The crowd noise subsided. Some people left and the others straggled slowly over to the bar and dining room of the resort.

Jimmy and I followed them in and took a corner table. He ordered an Old Milwaukee and I had a root beer. We looked across the table at each other and smiled. I lifted my glass and said, "From one old logger to a younger one, well done!"

He looked at me and said, "Aren't you the Dr. from across the lake? You were so calm, cool, and collected and knew just what and how to do what needed to be done." I smiled and said, "I am the 'Dr.' from across the lake and yet that wasn't exactly the person who got the job done. And besides, I couldn't have done it without you."

My mind drifted to all the incidents of my logging days when alone in the woods one had to be careful and creative. I shared some of my thoughts with Jimmy saying, "I'm sure you've had your near misses and scrapes." He nodded and said, "You are so right!"

I quoted a piece from Teilhard de Chardin's *Phenomenon of Man* about kindred spirits and said, "We would make a good pair of loggers."

He looked at me and said, "But you are a Dr. and I'm just a young logger."

I said, "You have no idea. My doctorate is in Philosophic and Social Foundations. It's not a medical degree. He looked at me and said, "Everybody thought you were a real Dr."

"Well, I can't be responsible for what people think. I can only do my best to help out. You just had a lesson in that. As the saying goes, *Don't think you know until you really know you know*."

Jimmy smiled, and said, "Now that does sound more like a philosopher."

We finished our drinks and I asked, if he had the time, if he could give me a ride home through the late remnants of the storm. I said, "It's just straight across the lake."

He said, "Sure, I'll just go back and pick up my tools and we can leave right away."

I said, "If you don't mind I'd like to come along and help you pick them up."

He said "okay" and we both stood up to leave.

The owner of the resort saw us leaving and met us at the door. He looked downcast and slowly raising his eyes he said, "We really thought he was dead. We really feel terrible about leaving him there."

"Don't worry," I said. "All things came together just in the right way and right time. By the way, I left a canoe beached down the shore. Could you take care of it for me until I can come back and get it?"

He smiled and nodded. "I'll take care of it." He added, "That must have been some crossing?"

I smiled and said, "It's one I will remember." He shook his head and walked back to the bar. I knew he was wondering, "Who was that old man anyway?"

We rode in silence back to the scene of the accident. We both stood on the road for a moment trying to assess the whole scene. The car must have smashed into the big pine that lay across the road and as it was sliding sideways had rolled over and smashed the top when it landed on the other side of the tree. Then the momentum just took it rolling down into the ditch and up against the big old aspen.

"They sure were lucky," Jimmy said. "You can see the roll marks where it hit three times before it came to a stop."

I nodded, saying, "We can only hope they'll all be okay." We returned to the task of unhooking the winches and picking up the axe, chain, and cant-hook. I smiled and said, "I spent many years using tools just like these."

Jimmy looked at me and said, "When was that?

I looked at him and smiled. "Many years ago I spent a lot of time when I was a young man working in the woods and I loved every moment of it."

Jimmy broke into a grin and offered, "I love it too. There is nothing like working in the woods and getting the job done all by yourself."

I smiled back and added, "I couldn't agree with you more, yet there were also times when someone else was there too. In my case my father came along and lent a welcome hand."

Jimmy sheepishly bobbed his head, grinning. "You've got that right. There were times when I was in a fix and Dad had to bail me out."

We traveled in silence as we threaded our way around the storm's leavings on the way to the other side of the lake. As we passed the boat landing we could appreciate the breadth and length of the lake. Jimmy offered, "I'll bet that really was some crossing." All I said was, "Yes, yes it was."

Then, with both of us lost in our own worlds, we continued on down around the south end of the lake and up the east shore past all of the places where I had spent so much time enjoying summers at the lake. Finally, we pulled up at the house and I slid off the four-wheeler. Turning to Jimmy I said, "It was a real pleasure sharing the day with you."

He looked at me and said, "You were more of an old logger than any Dr. I've ever seen. I enjoyed the day too." He swung aboard and waved as he headed back home.

I walked into the house and into the living room, right where I'd been standing when the guests from next door interrupted my musings. And then I collapsed in the old rocking chair in front of the big window overlooking the raging water and the wind-driven gray sky.

The late afternoon sun was beginning to break through the clouds and I reflected on the day's happenings. *"Just a logger" sums it all up pretty well*, I thought, as my mind returned to the memories of the day and those "other times" along the road of my life.

I must have dozed off, and awoke feeling a little chilly. I pulled several pieces of kindling and small logs from the old copper washtub near the fireplace and laid up a fire. Soon there were flames licking around the little logs. I wondered why I was so tired.

THE RULES FROM THE GAME OF LIFE:
A PLAYER'S MANUAL

Rule 1. Play One First (Be Myself)

I must be selfish and honest. This is the only REAL ME. There is only one of me. I must remember to play all of my cards in life's game and play them in order: 1. Self, 2. Mate, 3. Children, 4. Work, 5. Friends. If the cards are played out of order I am losing the game. If I am losing, those around me are losing, and the world is losing. (There are only three "must play" cards: 1, 4, and 5. Numbers 2 and 3 are "choice" cards.)

Rule 2. Stand Still in Silence

This enables me to see, feel, and be my real self. If I am afraid, the fear is mine. If I am angry, the anger is mine. If I am guilty, the guilt is mine. If I am lying, the lies are all mine. Any and all of the monsters (rocks)—all gifts of the past—fear, anger, guilt, and false pride are all mine NOW! I must release myself from these burdens. I must choose not to see the world through these dark glasses.

Rule 3. True, Not True—Mine, Not Mine

All things are what they are and they are either true or not true—mine or not mine. Ownership is essential. Only when I concentrate my energies on my own reality, can I come with my real self to the world.

Rule 4. Own it Now

The new gesture of our times—a fist clenched and held towards us and pulled sharply down as we say, "Yes!" We see this so often at sporting events—those other games of our times. This is done when something right has been

110

accomplished by either ourselves or someone else. I need to adopt this swift and definitive action. I must OWN IT NOW! Whatever the Truth might be, I must DO IT NOW!

Rule 5. Act in Love

Knowledge, care, responsibility, and respect will be my key watch words. I must develop an active concern for life and growth in all of my waking moments. It is only when you love others that you know that it is possible to love yourself. In fact you cannot have a love for self without a love for others. There is reciprocity in our nature that says yes to both truths in order to have either truth. Compassion must be the fire that lights your way into the world.

Rule 6. Dedicate Myself to Growth

I must become ("be" a person who "comes" into the world) dedicated to putting on my personhood. This is the only way that I can be open and free. Those four colors of my hood can only maintain their brilliance if there is growth in my intellect, my emotions, my body, and my spirit. I must remember that I will never know it all—and it doesn't matter. I must, however, continue to fill my cup (chalice or goblet) and share it with my brothers, my sisters, and the world.

Rule 7. Follow All of the Other Rules

In science when a proof is right (true) it is called elegant because it is so simple, so refined, and it fits perfectly into the grand design of things. This is my quest. This is my star. A holy endeavor is about to begin—the real me!

COROLLARIES TO THE RULES

Corollary One: Life Comes First

We have life. We must honor life. Human activity must always default to life. If there is any danger, we must immediately turn our attention to averting the danger by protecting and preserving life. Who, when upon hearing a child's call for help (aren't we all children?), would not respond? Be honest about life. We must be ready to hold life gently in our hands.

Corollary Two: Who Is Dead?

This is not a capricious statement. Unless somebody is dead, you'd better be following Rule 2. You need to do this in order to "see" more about whatever it is that has anybody doing anything but following Rule 2. It is a wake-up corollary to force the Truth of the Now into our thinking paradigm.

Corollary Three: True, and Doesn't Matter

This forces us to evaluate the significance of "whatever" in the Now. Many things are true, but have little if any meaning for us right this minute. We should be "doing" the Truth of One in the Now. This is all that matters. Some will say he, she, it hurt me. True, but doesn't matter now—right this minute—even if there is permanent and irreparable damage; the Truth stays the same in the Now. Some will also say, "If I go home he, she, it will hurt me." If true—Rule 4—Own it now! Don't go home.

Corollary Four: No Blood—No Bones, It Doesn't Matter

This says, "No life-threatening thing is going on right now." We will immediately get to the Truth of life. If life is not at risk we have time to follow Rule 2. This is especially beneficial when raising children.

Corollary Five: Whose Is That?

Really anything, everything, is either mine or not mine. This helps us to be really honest with Rule 3 (True–Not True, Mine–Not Mine). Don't touch anything that is not true and not yours!

The Rules are from *The Game of Life: A Player's Manual For Executives and others,* by Don Davison, Ph.D. (Zirahuen Publishers, ©1995, 2005, 2009, 2011, 2017, http://amzn.to/fOrqEi).